# Simple Thoughts That Can Literally Change Your Life

# Simple Thoughts That Can Literally Change Your Life

A one-of-a-kind collection of positive, inspiring words

Edited by
Douglas Pagels

**Blue Mountain Press**™
Boulder, Colorado

Cover photo © Chaluntorn Preeyasombat / 500px.
Interior images used under license from Shutterstock.com.

Library of Congress Control Number: 2017948024
ISBN: 978-1-68088-191-2

▌and Blue Mountain Press are registered in U.S. Patent and Trademark Office.
Certain trademarks are used under license.

Printed in China.
First Printing: 2017

✿ This book is printed on recycled paper.

This book is printed on paper that has been specially produced to be acid free (neutral pH) and contains no groundwood or unbleached pulp. It conforms with the requirements of the American National Standards Institute, Inc., so as to ensure that this book will last and be enjoyed by future generations.

**Blue Mountain Arts, Inc.**
P.O. Box 4549, Boulder, Colorado 80306

# Contents

# So much
# is possible

Each day is a blank page in the diary of your life. The secret of success is in turning that diary into the best story you possibly can.

——

Douglas Pagels

You know all those things you've always wanted to do? You should go do them.

——

Author Unknown

I see life as a tremendous gift. Every morning you wake up to fantastic possibilities. I would like to spend the rest of my life realizing those possibilities. I want to learn and to grow. I want to experience; I want to understand; I want to love, care, and share. I want to do all the marvelous things that are available.

———

Leo Buscaglia

Embrace the gift you've been given... and let the adventure begin.

———

Douglas Pagels

Choose to be happy and positive.
Live like the blessed human you are.

———

Beyoncé

You're an original, an individual, a masterpiece.
Celebrate that; don't let your uniqueness make
you shy. Don't be someone other than the wonder
you are. Every star is important to the sky.

———

Douglas Pagels

The closer we get to being who we are meant to be, the brighter we shine.

———

Author Unknown

# Believe in yourself

I have a problem with low self-esteem — which is really ridiculous when you consider how amazing I am.

Author Unknown

One reason we struggle with insecurity: we're comparing our behind the scenes to everyone else's highlight reel.

Steven Furtick

Don't underestimate me. I know more than I say, think more than I speak, and notice more than you realize.

———

Author Unknown

I am aware that I am less than some people prefer me to be, but most people are unaware that I am so much more than what they see.

———

Douglas Pagels

You are never taller than when
you stand up for yourself.

Author Unknown

If you have never loved yourself, never really loved yourself, gently and unconditionally, now is the time to do that. Love yourself, forgive yourself, and at the same time know that there is nothing to forgive... Unconditional love can do some amazing things, and it's a real safety net. And we can do amazing things when we know that we are safe.

———

Max Navarre

Remember, you have nothing to prove. Be yourself and enjoy.

———

Susan RoAne

Who you are is more than enough. Take a flower and how it grows. It doesn't grow according to someone else's idea of what it should be. It grows in accordance with the perfect pattern that is inside it. It doesn't try to grow from the outside in, but from the inside out. It allows the potential to unfold in its own way.

———

Ernie Carwile

Don't stress out by comparing yourself with others. The simple truth is... some people are always going to seem better and others will always seem worse. It's okay. We're all different. That's pretty much the way the world works.

———

Douglas Pagels

# Words to
# wake up to

"Then what is it?" asked Owl.
"It's today," squeaked Piglet.
"My favorite day," said Pooh.

———

Benjamin Hoff


When you start each day with a grateful heart,
the light illuminates from within.

———

Author Unknown

Choose to shine.

Author Unknown

You did not wake up today to be mediocre.

Author Unknown

Each morning when I open my eyes I say to myself: I, not events, have the power to make me happy or unhappy today. I can choose which it shall be.

Groucho Marx

All happiness depends on a leisurely breakfast.

John Gunther

Drink some coffee and pretend you know what you're doing.

Author Unknown

# Plan on amazing things happening

You were once wild here. Don't let them tame you.

Isadora Duncan

Dabble on the wild side. Rummage through your child side. Let wonder and innocence take you to the park to try on the shiny new roller skates of instinct. Something in you knows how to glide. It doesn't come with planning or foresight or lots of furrows on your brow. It comes with a squeal and a direction for now.

———

Tama J. Kieves

I think it would help if every now and then I let the child that shines within me live in harmony with the adult I'm required to be.

———

Douglas Pagels

You don't have to be *the* best; you just have to do *your* best.

———

Cameron Diaz

We're not here to be average. We're here to be awesome.

———

Author Unknown

You are personally responsible for so much of the sunshine that brightens up your life. Optimists and gentle souls continually benefit from their very own versions of daylight saving time. They get extra hours of happiness and sunshine every day.

———

Douglas Pagels

This is the part where you get a little reminder of how amazing your days can be! The more you plant the seeds of creativity, spontaneity, adventure, and delight, the more you get to enjoy the fruits of life.

———

Douglas Pagels


You have to do what others won't to achieve what others don't.

———

Author Unknown

# Introduction

I'm a lover of words. I've had a number of times in my life when the perfect words, woven together into a short saying or an encouraging quotation, have had much more of an impact on me than entire books.

I've relied on quotes many times as a parent, when my children needed a little extra hope or help. And as a friend who is sometimes at a loss for words of encouragement, I have shared bits of wisdom I've heard from others — far wiser than I — to help light the way.

Writers, from both very contemporary times and from long ago, sometimes give you the impression they're writing with a magic wand instead of a pen when they put together brief phrases that overflow with inspiration. I love finding those gems hidden among all the words circulating around the world. One finds them best not by just surfing online, but by diving into research as I have done in different countries and for dozens of years... poring endlessly through stacks of books in libraries, leaning on the shelves of good old-fashioned bookstores until the wee hours, and simply being open to all the possibilities.

Somewhere in this book there is a quote — or ten or twelve of them — that speaks directly to you, lifts up your heart, and inspires your life. Find those words and hold on to them as though they were treasures, because — indeed — that is exactly what they are.

— Douglas Pagels

Some of the secret joys of living are not found by rushing from point A to point B, but by slowing down and inventing some imaginary letters along the way.

Douglas Pagels

# Random notes and favorite quotes

Everything is figureoutable.

———

Author Unknown

Whatever is good for the soul... do that.

———

Author Unknown

Your creative energies often can be ignited by two words.

*What's next?*

———

Nido R. Qubein

I'd like to live in a country where the official motto was, "You never know." It would help me relax.

———

George Carlin

# Be the
# reason someone
# smiles today

You can't keep a person out of the rain, but you can hold an umbrella for them and just let them know you care.

Author Unknown

Be kind. Everyone you meet is fighting a hard battle.

———

John Watson

Resolve to be: tender with the young, compassionate with the aged, sympathetic with the striving, and tolerant of the weak and the wrong. There will be times in your life when you are all of these.

———

Author Unknown

Kindness is free. Sprinkle that stuff everywhere.

———

Author Unknown

If there are children in the circle of your life, help them be happy. Listen to them. Laugh with them. Teach them to fill their hearts with feelings of wonder and to be full of courage and hope. Help them live strong. Inspire them by telling them of remarkable things. And whenever they wonder if it's worthwhile to dream, remind them that there are footprints on the moon — and that, yes, a person's highest hopes *really can* come true.

———

Douglas Pagels

Go out of your way to be good to an older person. You'll discover that you can make somebody's entire day with a smile, a phone call, some fresh-picked daisies, or whatever it is you've got.

Our elders have so much to give to those who listen, but they are the ones who deserve to receive. Don't pass up the chance to brighten their lives. An old adage reminds us that they need only a little, but they need that little — a lot.

———

Douglas Pagels

# And make sure
# one of those smiling
# faces is yours

When life gives you a hundred reasons
to cry, show life that you have a thousand
reasons to smile.

Author Unknown

Happiness is the best facelift.

Joni Mitchell

Smile. Happy looks good on you.

---

Author Unknown

If it's not fun, you're not doing it right.

Bob Basso

Happy people have sparkly eyes.

A young child's observation

I want you to have times when you just simply delight in life.

Douglas Pagels

Too many people put off something that brings them joy....

I got to thinking one day about all those women on the Titanic who passed up dessert at dinner that fateful night in an effort to cut back. From then on, I've tried to be a little more flexible.

———

Erma Bombeck


You can't buy happiness. But you can buy cupcakes. And that's sort of the same thing.

———

Author Unknown

# On friends

$A$ friend is one of the nicest things you can have — and one of the best things you can be.

Douglas Pagels

Life is all about finding people who are your kind of crazy.

Author Unknown

Surround yourself with people who get you.

Author Unknown

The best portion of your life will be the small, nameless moments you spend smiling with someone who matters to you.

Author Unknown

My friendships are a strength that I know I can rely on. When I have true, meaningful friendships in my life, I know I have the support to handle anything that comes my way. I've always thought that friends are the angels that are sent down to help you along life's path. They bring encouragement, understanding, strength, fun, and laughter.

———

Miranda Kerr

When you're young, hang out with old people. When you're old, hang out with young people. When you're in the middle, hang out with both.

———

Maria Menounos

Find your tribe. Love them hard.

———

Author Unknown

# On family

"There is nothing more important than family."
Those words should be etched in stone on the
sidewalks that lead to every home.

Douglas Pagels

Families are what you make them.

Author Unknown

Please excuse the mess. Our family is busy
making memories.

Author Unknown

We may not have it all together, but together we have it all.

Author Unknown

# Life can be
# so wonder-full

*ᔑᔑᔑᔑᔑ*

This much is certain: life is amazing if one is paying attention.

———

Dr. Robin R. Meyers

There are two ways to live your life. One is as though nothing is a miracle. The other is as though everything is a miracle.

———

Albert Einstein

Everything is miraculous. It is a miracle that one does not melt in one's bath.

Picasso

Wonder comes in all shapes and sizes, at any place and in any moment of the day....

If you stop to consider the moments in which you've come across wonder, you recognize the aura that comes with such experiences. It's as if, once you take in the miracle of it, your next breath is a bit more sacred.

Jan Goldstein

She loved her life and it loved her right back.

Author Unknown

Optimist: Someone who figures that taking a step backward after taking a step forward is not a disaster, it's a cha-cha.

Robert Brault

If you have the choice between a la-di-da life and an ooh-la-la one, well... you know what to do.

Choose the one that requires you to dust off your dancing shoes.

Douglas Pagels

# If I had my life to live over

I'd dare to make more mistakes next time. I'd relax, I would limber up. I would be sillier than I have been this trip. I would take fewer things seriously. I would take more chances. I would climb more mountains and swim more rivers. I would eat more ice cream and less beans. I would perhaps have more actual troubles, but I'd have fewer imaginary ones.

You see, I'm one of those people who live sensibly and sanely, hour after hour, day after day. Oh, I've had my moments, and if I had it to do over again, I'd have more of them....

In fact, I'd try to have nothing else. Just moments, one after another, instead of living so many years ahead of each day. I've been one of those persons who never goes anywhere without a thermometer, a hot-water bottle, a raincoat and a parachute. If I had to do it again, I would travel lighter than I have.

If I had my life to live over, I would start barefoot earlier in the spring and stay that way later in the fall. I would go to more dances. I would ride more merry-go-rounds. I would pick more daisies.

———

Author Unknown

It's never too late to be what you
might have been.

———

George Eliot

Each person's task in life is to become an
increasingly better person.

———

Leo Tolstoy

My goal in life is to become the kind of person my dog thinks I am.

Author Unknown

# Stand your ground

For much of my life I was run by this nagging voice in the back of my head that kept insisting, "You're not doing enough! You're not doing enough!" But now I'm starting to listen to my body a lot more. It needs tender loving care and I'm the only one who can provide that.

Leonard Felder, PhD

And every day, the world will drag you by the hand, yelling, "This is important! And this is important! And this is important! You need to worry about this! And this! And this!"

And each day, it's up to you to yank your hand back, put it on your heart and say, "No. This is what's important."

———

Iain Thomas

Whatever you decide to do,
make sure it makes you happy.

Author Unknown

I may be uncertain about exactly where I'm headed, but I am very clear regarding this:

I'm glad I've got a ticket to go on this magnificent journey.

———

Douglas Pagels

Life is short. In choosing a path make sure you first identify those things that you can do. Then, reduce your choice further by zooming in on what you *really* want to do. Finally, select those things that you *really, really* want to do — and then do them.

———

Ohad Kamin

# If you've got your health, you've got everything

~~~~~~~~~

If you wear out your body, where are you going to live?

You only get one, and it has to last you a long time, so it's important to learn sooner, rather than later, how to take care of this wonderful human machine we have.

———

J. Victor McGuire, PhD

When was the last time you did something to better yourself?

———

Author Unknown

January is a great time to start anew with healthy habits, but so is May. September works, too. And you don't have to start a healthy habit on the first of the month or on a Monday. Anytime you can make a change that will make your life healthier is a good time.

———

Winnie Abramson, ND

If I don't do me, I don't get done.

———

Jacquelyn Small

When you stroll along and unwind outside under a great big beautiful sky, you can actually walk your worries away.

Douglas Pagels

You have a choice. You can throw in the towel — or you can use it to wipe the sweat off your face before you continue on.

Author Unknown

I think you should just go for it.

Author Unknown

Exercise in the morning before your brain figures out what you're doing.

Author Unknown

# Sweet dreams
# are made of this

I'm just a girl, standing in front of a salad, asking it to be a donut.

Author Unknown

The food you eat can either be the safest and most powerful form of medicine or the slowest form of poison.

Ann Wigmore

Every time you eat, you have the opportunity to invest in your health. So you should eat the healthiest foods you can find and afford.

———

Winnie Abramson, ND

Eating well is a form of self-respect.

———

Author Unknown

# More random notes and favorite quotes

Karma has no menu. You get served what you deserve.

Author Unknown

Never assume that loud is strong and quiet is weak.

Author Unknown

If "Plan A" didn't work, the alphabet has twenty-five more letters. Stay cool.

Author Unknown

No, we don't always get what we want. But consider this: there are people who will never have what you have right now.

Author Unknown

Get clear on why you're chasing what you're chasing.

Author Unknown

You are what you do, not what you say you'll do.

Author Unknown

If the desire to write is not accompanied by actual writing, then the desire is not to write.

Hugh Prather

# Try to be positive

The most important decision you can make is to be in a good mood.

Voltaire

Tell that negative committee that meets inside your head to sit down and shut up.

Author Unknown

Be optimistic about as many things as possible, realistic about things requiring an exact, matter-of-fact outlook, and pessimistic about absolutely nothing at all.

Douglas Pagels

# You have your life,
# they have theirs;
# be okay with that

You wouldn't worry so much about what others think of you if you realized how seldom they do.

*Eleanor Roosevelt*

Every time we start thinking we're the center of the universe, the universe turns around and says with a slightly distracted air, "I'm sorry. What'd you say your name was again?"

*Margaret Maron*

People aren't ignoring you. They are busy with their own lives. And the way to stop feeling ignored is to get busy with yours.

Author Unknown

Worry gives small things a big shadow.

Swedish Proverb

Keep your face always toward the sunshine.

Walt Whitman

# And as for work: your job is to keep things in perspective

Sometimes it's important to work for that pot of gold. But other times it's essential to take time off and to make sure that your most important decision in the day simply consists of choosing which color to slide down on the rainbow.

———

Douglas Pagels

One of the symptoms of approaching nervous breakdown is the belief that one's work is terribly important.

———

Bertrand Russell

Fill your life with adventures, not things. Have stories to tell, not stuff to show.

———

Author Unknown

When it comes to enjoying life and making use of who we are, all of us *can*; it's just that some of us *don't*.

———

Benjamin Hoff

Act as if what you do makes a difference. It does.

———

William James

As long as we are alive and kicking, we can be improving ourselves. No matter our age, if we always have a project to which we can apply ourselves, then we will wake up every day with an objective, something productive to get done. This allows us to go to bed at night in the peaceful knowledge that we have done some good, gained some achievement, however small. Having ears for this lesson has been one of the luckiest pieces of listening I've done.

Nick Offerman

Having a wish list... is good.

Having a checklist... is great.

Douglas Pagels

# It's good
# for the soul to be
# truly grateful

When it comes to life, the critical thing is whether you take things for granted or take them with gratitude.

———

G. K. Chesterton

The things you take for granted... someone else is praying for.

———

Author Unknown

When your heart is filled with gratitude for what you do have, your head isn't nearly so worried about what you don't.

———

Douglas Pagels

Gratitude is everything... Being grateful helps create a positive attitude. Gratitude shifts your focus from what you don't have to all that you do have. I try my best to live from the point of gratitude, which means focusing on the positives, and share my life and its rewards when I can.

Miranda Kerr


Gratitude turns what we have into enough.

Author Unknown

Things that are very important to say:

Please.
(upon rising)

Thank you.
(upon retiring)

———

Author Unknown

If the only prayer you say in your whole life is "thank you," that would suffice.

———

Johannes Meister Eckhart

# Don't text me about this

Just a reminder for the folks who haven't figured this out yet: if they turn off their smart phones and power down their devices a little more often, they can spend more time with full-size, real-life, laughing, lovely people. I know this is no small task, but it's kind of a big deal.

— Douglas Pagels

Consider the rapaciousness of our online activity. By 2012, we were asking Google to help us find things more than a trillion times each year (in a remarkable 146 languages). We were also sending one another 144 billion emails — every day. In 2013, we "liked" 4.5 billion items on Facebook every day... Every second, we uploaded 637 photos to Instagram....

The sheer volume of time we devote to our devices means we each are carving "expendable" hours away from other parts of our lives.

———

Michael Harris

Social media is not real life.

———

Author Unknown


For fast-acting relief, try slowing down.

———

Jane Wagner

Every conversation I had seemed to eventually come around to the same dilemmas we are all facing — the stress of over-busyness, overworking, overconnecting on social media, and underconnecting with ourselves and with one another. The space, the gaps, the pauses, the silence — those things that allow us to regenerate and recharge — had all but disappeared....

It seemed to me that the people who were genuinely thriving in their lives were the ones who had made room for well-being, wisdom, wonder, and giving.

Arianna Huffington

Practice taking your time as often as you can... For those of us who spend a lot of time online, this may mean reining in an overactive social media existence. I was once on the social media "hamster wheel," but I let it go. It's kind of amazing how much less busy I feel, and how much extra time I've freed up to do other things that are more important to me.

———

Winnie Abramson, ND


Once she stopped rushing through life, she was amazed how much more life she had time for.

———

Author Unknown

You can't Google this, but you can *goggle* it.
(And *water wing* it too.)

Giving in to peer pressure is never a good thing.
But giving in to *pier* pressure — almost always is.

———

Douglas Pagels

# Choose wisely

Life is about making choices. That's pretty much what it boils down to.

Robin Roberts

You're always one decision away from a totally different life.

Author Unknown

Decisions are incredibly important things!
Good decisions will come back to bless you. Bad
decisions can come back to haunt you. That's why
it's so important that you take the time to choose
wisely. Choose to do the things that will reflect
well... on your ability, your integrity, your spirit,
your health, your tomorrows, your smiles, your
dreams, and yourself.

There is someone who will thank you for doing
the things you do now with foresight and wisdom
and respect. It's the person you will someday
be. You have a chance to make that person so
thankful and so proud. And all you have to do is...
choose wisely.

———

Douglas Pagels

# The present is
# such a gift

What a wonderful life I've had! I only wish I'd realized it sooner.

Colette

Whether you're eighteen or eighty, I encourage you to be both thankful for — and aware of — the precious day you're living in. There's always more to appreciate in the present moment than we realize. Believe me: years from now, the truth of this will shine. And, looking back, one of your sincere regrets will be not knowing how good you had it... at the time.

Douglas Pagels

Life is short, and it's up to you to make it sweet.

Sadie Delany

# We are
# all travelers on
# remarkable journeys

I don't want to get to the end of my life and find that I just lived the length of it. I want to have lived the width of it as well.

*Diane Ackerman*

I saw a car with a bumper sticker that read, "The one who dies with the most toys wins." I think it should have said joys.

*Tama J. Kieves*

I didn't have the time,
   but I made time.
I didn't have the knowledge,
   but I did what I knew.
I didn't have the support,
   but I learned to support myself.
I didn't have the confidence,
   but the confidence came with results.
I had a lot going against me,
   but I had enough going for me.

————

Author Unknown


Take pride in how far you have come, and have
faith in how far you can go.

————

Author Unknown

# From this moment on

I hope that somewhere out there this book will remind other gypsies on a trail of where they are and what they should be doing.

———

Jimmy Buffett

We close the book when the story ends, then
we open our hearts to all the possibilities...
and the real story begins.

Douglas Pagels

# ACKNOWLEDGMENTS

We gratefully acknowledge the permission granted by the following authors, publishers, and authors' representatives to reprint poems or excerpts from their publications:

Echo Point Books and Media for "I see life as a tremendous gift" by Leo Buscaglia from *Success Secrets of the Motivational Superstars* by Michael Jeffreys. Copyright © 2013 by Michael Jeffreys. All rights reserved.

Beyoncé Knowles and Shure Media for "Choose to be happy…" from *The Best Advice I Ever Got* by Katie Couric. Copyright © 2011 by Beyoncé Knowles. All rights reserved.

Steven Furtick for "One reason we struggle with insecurity: we're comparing our behind the scenes to everyone else's highlight reel." (May 10, 2011, 15:58 UTC). [Tweet].

HarperCollins Publishers for "Remember, you have nothing…" from *How to Work a Room* by Susan RoAne. Copyright © 2000 by Susan RoAne. All rights reserved. And for "You don't have to be…" from *The Body Book* by Cameron Diaz with Sandra Bark. Copyright © 2014 by Cameron Diaz. All rights reserved. And for "When you're young…" from *The Everygirl's Guide to Life* by Maria Menounos. Copyright © 2011 by Maria Menounos. All rights reserved. And for "For fast-acting relief…" from *The Search for Intelligent Life in the Universe* by Jane Wagner. Copyright © 1986 by Jane Wagner, Inc. All rights reserved.

Verbena Pond Publishing Company for "Who you are is more than…" from *Chipped but Not Broken* by Ernie Carwile. Copyright © 2006 by Ernie Carwile, Inc. All rights reserved.

Dutton, an imprint of Penguin Publishing Group, a division of Penguin Random House LLC, for "'Then what is it?' asked Owl" and "When it comes to enjoying…" from *The Tao of Pooh* by Benjamin Hoff, illustrated by Ernest H. Shepard. Copyright © 1982 by Benjamin Hoff. All rights reserved. And for "As long as we are alive…" from *Paddle Your Own Canoe: One Man's Fundamentals for Delicious Living* by Nick Offerman. Copyright © 2014 by Nick Offerman. All rights reserved.

Charles H. Kerr Publishing Company for "You were once wild…" by Isadora Duncan from *Isadora Speaks: Writings and Speeches of Isadora Duncan*, edited and introduced by Franklin Rosemont. Copyright © 1994 by Charles H. Kerr Publishing Company. All rights reserved.

Tarcher, an imprint of Penguin Publishing Group, a division of Penguin Random House LLC, and Tama Kieves, www.TamaKieves.com, for "Dabble on the wild side" and "I saw a car with…" from *This Time I Dance: Trusting the Journey of Creating the Work You Love* by Tama J. Kieves. Copyright © 2002 by Tama J. Kieves. All rights reserved.

Sourcebooks, Inc., for "Your creative energies often…" from *Daily Motivation: 365 Messages to Inspire You at Work and in Life* by Nido R. Qubein. Copyright © 2016 by Nido R. Qubein. All rights reserved.

Hyperion, a division of Hachette Book Group, Inc., for "I'd like to live in a country…" from *Brain Droppings* by George Carlin. Copyright © 1997 by Comedy Concepts, Inc. All rights reserved. And for "Life is about making choices" from *From the Heart: Seven Rules to Live By* by Robin Roberts. Copyright © 2007 by Robin René Roberts. All rights reserved.

Joni Mitchell for "Happiness is the best facelift" from "Facelift" from the album *Taming the Tiger*. Copyright © 1998 by Joni Mitchell. All rights reserved.

The Estate of Erma Bombeck and the Aaron Priest Literary Agency for "Too many people put off…" from *Forever, Erma: Best-Loved Writing from America's Favorite Humorist* by Erma Bombeck. Copyright © 1996 by the Estate of Erma Bombeck. All rights reserved. Reprinted by permission.

Hay House, www.hayhouse.com.au, for "My friendships are a…" and "Gratitude is everything…" from *Treasure Yourself: Power Thoughts for My Generation* by Miranda Kerr. Copyright © 2010 by Miranda Kerr. All rights reserved.

Doubleday Religion, an imprint of the Crown Publishing Group, a division of Penguin Random House LLC, for "This much is certain…" from *Morning Sun on a White Piano* by Robin Meyers. Copyright © 1998 by Dr. Robin R. Meyers. All rights reserved.

Red Wheel/Weiser, LLC, Newburyport, MA, www.redwheelweiser.com, for "Wonder comes in all shapes…" from *Life Can Be This Good* by Jan Goldstein. Copyright © 2002 by Jan Goldstein. All rights reserved.